I0456624

Sampler of
Miraculous
Interventions™
Series, I - VIII
by Deborah Aubrey-Peyron

Home Crafted Artistry & Printing
Lanesville, IN 47111

Home Crafted Artistry & Printing
2404 Scenic Drive NE, #6, Lanesville IN 47136
e-mail: HomeCraftedArtistry@yahoo.com
e-mail: peyronsinjesus@yahoo.com
Cover design by Mary Dow Bibb Smith and Deborah Aubrey-Peyron
Photographs are author's family photos

TABLE OF CONTENTS

"...whatsoever ye do,

do all to the glory of God."

I Cor 10:31b KJV

Miraculous Interventions™

Deborah Aubrey-Peyron
With Contributions
from Mark Peyron and Ben Merk

True life stories of miraculous events that have shaped the author's life and those she has known.

HELP!

Many times in my life I have heard, for lack of a better word, a "guardian angel" speak. It has always been a male voice, audible, outside of my head. It has brought warnings, healing or healing words, instructions, whatever was necessary at the time.

The first time I can remember a clairaudient event, I was about nine years old. I was at a friend's house after school, down in her basement, watching television with her. I heard, *"Go upstairs now!"* It was a command!

I jumped up and ran upstairs. Her mother Kathleen was on the phone and couldn't get off. Her skillet was about to catch fire! She hollered, "Debbie, pull that skillet off the stove!" I grabbed a potholder and moved the skillet to the side.

I went back downstairs to watch TV again with Karen. She asked me where I went. I replied that her mother needed my help upstairs. She then asked me how I knew, but by that time, I was already engrossed in our afternoon soap-opera.

WAIT FOR IT!

After my divorce from Clarence, my boys and I still managed to do nice things. We went on a few trips, vacations, day excursions to the local amusement park in the summer and fall, picnics and family nights. We made joyful times to help us all heal. When my boys were growing up, the amusement park in the summer was their favorite place to go! I'd make sandwiches and drinks, and off we'd go, over the river to the city for a day of fun in the sun at the pool, park and rides.

We'd usually start pool side where it wasn't so crowded. The boys would race around the Lazy River. I would paddle and take my time, relaxing. There was a strong undercurrent that kept the water flowing around the river. When you got to the area where you got out, the current was strong enough to knock a person over if you were not careful.

While I was still going around the river with the boys being way ahead of me racing each other, I saw a lovely picture playing out in front of me. A mother was on her raft with a little boy, maybe 18 months old, in her lap. He had the look of a Downs Syndrome baby. He was trying to lap up the water. Momma was ever so gently stopping him every time. It was an adorable picture. At the time I wondered at this significance but gave God thanks for it anyway.

When it came this lady's turn for getting out of the pool, she was ahead of me. I had just gotten to the area as she was stepping out. The water was maybe two and a half feet where she was and over four feet out where I was.

All of a sudden in my spirit, out loud like someone was standing next to me, I heard, "*Stop, wait for it!*"

Then I saw as in slow motion, the baby slip from his mother's arms down into the water, being sucked down into the undercurrent, out to the river area. I heard again, out loud, *"**Wait for it!**"* I saw the baby going deeper and deeper under the water, heading straight for me. The frantic mother was fighting, trying to get through the crowd. Then I heard *"**Now! Now!**"* I dove down into the water, grabbed the baby and came up.

He blew out bubbles, sputtered and squirmed in my arms. He was okay! The mother came running in the water as fast as she could towards us. I popped that baby on my other hip with a strong grip on him, held out my hand and said, "Calm down!"

She was visibly crying, "I'm not mad at him! I couldn't get all those x'!*# people to move!"

I handed her baby back to her and he immediately tried to wiggle out of her arms. She exited the pool quickly, baby in her arms, and said not one word of thanks to me. It's okay. The safe baby was thanks enough for me.

WARNING!

When Mark and I were first married, maybe not quite two years, all the boys were living with us. We were a lively household. I worked part time so I could be home when the kids got off the bus after school.

One day I came in shortly after the guys got home. Ben had given a ride to someone he met at the local coffee shop. I came through the living room and saw this man in the kitchen. Up until then, anyone our children had brought over as friends we treated as family. Hello! How are ya! Nice to meet you. Are you hungry?

Not this time. This boy looked at me, and I stopped. He was dark, and I don't mean his color. There was black all around him. I said to my son, "Ben, honey, can I see you in the back bedroom?"

He said, "Sure Momma."

I stayed very calm.

"Son, you have to get this man out of our house. Lose him. Make sure he can never find his way back here again. I've never told you that you can't have a friend, but not this one, son."

He nodded his head yes, walked into the kitchen and said, "Come on, we have to leave."

About five years later, this man went on a killing spree. He killed several family members while robbing them. He is in prison for life.

When God sends you messages, inclinations, or warnings, heed them.

It may well save your life.

13

VISIONARY

This happened in the fall of 2007. We were having friends over for dinner. I walked to the back bedroom to call the boys for dinner. I was standing in their doorway when I felt the house jolt. Hard! It was as if something had just slammed into the earth! Not an earthquake, but a moving of the whole planet! I screamed. At this point, I did not realize I was seeing in the Spirit and not in the flesh. Within two seconds everything in my sight turned upside down, the whole room and everything. I saw Mark and Andy fall off their beds and onto the floor. I saw their beds fall down on top of them. I screamed again and bent to my knees onto the floor, not knowing which way was up. I screamed again, "Did you feel that? Did you see that?"

The boys were scared then. Andy cried out, "What's wrong, Momma!"

I said again, "Didn't you feel that? The earth moved!" I knew something was coming!

I worried over this. I wondered if this was prophesy for the year 2012, or whether this was a personal prophesy for me. During that time we did have a tremendous upheaval in our lives with the loss of my job and the financial stress it put us under.

That spring, Mark and I went to Mary's Farm in Southern Indiana. There was a priest there who was a visionary. I told him my experience. He said it was God's way of warning us about what was going to happen. He said God knew it would turn my world upside down...

...but what if there was a larger warning contained in this vision, about a comet on its way to earth?

Miraculous Interventions™ II
Modern Day Priests, Prophets, Pastors & Everyday Visionaries

Deborah Aubrey-Peyron

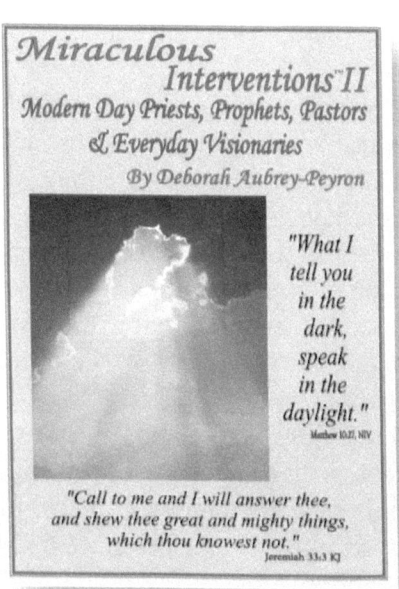

Amazing stories from various pastors, lay ministers and those who are called to walk in the office of the miraculous - their experiences with the Lord and the divine interventions they have witnessed.

INTRODUCTION

Many people in their lifetimes, if they know one true miracle worker besides Jesus Christ, they consider themselves very blessed. What are the odds of one person being close friends with many true miracle workers scattered everywhere from Seattle, Washington to Orlando, Florida?

That is an interesting question. Maybe it was because our spirits recognized each other's spirits, and in that way we became close. We just drug our flesh along for the ride. I am not talking about "celebrity" pastors on the television (nothing against television evangelists). I am talking about everyday visionaries. These people, whom I have had the privilege of calling friends, are out on the streets or in small home churches, calling people to God the Father, Jesus Christ and the Holy Spirit.

They have called people utilizing God's miracles, signs and wonders and with visions and gifts of the Holy Spirit. He is calling all to Christ no matter where they sit in a pew on a Saturday or a Sunday.

Having sat and listened to them tell their stories, and writing them down, has been a wonderful treat for me. Not only have they fascinating stories to tell, but how they were called by God are stories in themselves. Even how I met each individual is another fine narrative.

For me, this is a more enjoyable book to have written than my first one. Not necessarily easier; just not so much about me. These were whole new adventures to go on just by turning the page. How exciting! Let's get started. My hope is that you enjoy our journey too!

Welcome to "Miraculous Interventions II."

Shalom,

Deborah Aubrey-Peyron, Author

MEDJUGORJE
Father Bernie Weber

Father Bernie stated he was in Medjugorje in 1987, a place he really didn't want to go to. This is his story of how God got him there.

In 1987, while at a local parish, Father Bernie was being "pestered" by a couple who had just come back from the Medjugorje shrine. They thought he should make a pilgrimage to Yugoslavia. It was not in his heart to go. But, after a time, he told them he would go back to the rectory and pray before a big creosote cross. (An 8 x 8 railroad tie size cross). He "put out a fleece". He said, "If I stand in front of the cross and the moon is on the other side of the cross, that's a sign from God and I'll go to Medjugorje."

Well, the moon was behind his back and he was facing the cross. He said to himself, "Good, I don't have to go to Medjugorje."

As he was walking back to his rectory the Lord spoke to him. The Lord God said, *"THAT'S NO SIGN. WRITE YOUR PROVINCIAL."*

This took him by surprise. But in obedience he wrote a letter that was not very encouraging. In fact, it was a pretty neutral letter. He expected to get a letter back saying something like, "It's not approved by the church, it's nonsense, etc." Father Bernie did not want to go to Yugoslavia. He reasoned, "The Blessed Mother is right here. Why should I have to go all the way over there?"

The provincial wrote back. He not only allowed Father Bernie to go but encouraged him to go! Father Bernie's reply was? "Aaaaahhhh!!" But what could he say? So he went.

While there, he met a couple who agreed with his ministry of healing. They started sending him people to be prayed over. *Everyone* they sent to him was healed!

Now the church had not yet given its official approval. One of the laymen involved with Our Lady of Fatima was there. He was a Fatima Crusader, and they were adamantly opposed to Medjugorje because the pope had yet to consecrate it with the Bishops of Russia. And in their eyes, every disaster that was happening in the land was because this hadn't been consecrated yet.

This man and his wife came to see Father Bernie at 10:30 in the evening. They came to where Bernie was staying. He said to him, "Father Bernie, there is an Irish lady with bad knees. She has had to cancel all her visitations to the Marian shrine because she can't walk to them. Would you go over and please pray for her?"

"Alright."

Father Bernie went over to where she was staying. There was a courtyard there with a lot of people in it. It just so happened they met a Croatian man who lived in the United States. He spoke perfect English and perfect Croatian. The couple invited him to come along with them. Father Bernie prayed over the Irish lady. Her knees were healed in front of the Fatima Crusader and the Croatian man. Now, she could continue making her visitation to the Marian Center.

There was another man there, an Englishman. He also had bad knees. Father Bernie asked him if he needed prayer. The Englishman replied very stoically, "No, that's alright Father. You have more important things to do."

"Okay."

While Father was still making this pilgrimage, there was a set of grandparents living at the house where he was staying. They had a son who was married and had a little three-year-old girl. The grandmother asked through a translator, "Would you pray over my three-year-old granddaughter? She has never walked in her life." That was all they told him.

"Sure."

18

It was quite cool out and the little child had on several layers of clothing. The mother was holding her. They were all outside gathered around, the mother, father, the grandparents, Father Bernie, the interpreter and the little girl.

Father Bernie put his hand on the little girl's hair but she didn't like that. He then put his hand on her back. While they were praying he felt heat coming out of her back, through all the layers of clothing and into his hand! When they got through praying, through the translator, Father told the little girl's mother to squat down with her. He told the father to do the same. He was a little distance from his wife and daughter. Then, he told the father, to call his daughter.

The mother let go of the child and she waddled all on her own to the father. They all started crying. They all went into praising God. Everyone started shouting, "It's a miracle! It's a miracle!" Later on, the little girl was standing all by herself playing with the hair on her head. The grandmother started yelling in Croatian. The translator translated the grandmother's outburst. "Look! She could never do that before!" She had never even stood on her own.

Afterwards, Father Bernie found out the reason she had never walked before. At six months old, she had spinal meningitis. It ate away the myelin film around the spinal cord. All the electrical signals got shorted out going down the branch to the legs. The signals never got to the legs so she couldn't walk. She couldn't stand at all for three years before that day. Father Bernie continued his story, "When I felt heat go down her back that was God healing the myelin so fast that heat came out. And that's why she could walk now. Within five minutes, she was running."

This was a level four miracle.

SHOE BOXES
Pastor Ivie Dennis

It was Christmas time, December of 2004. The Board of Lifeline Outreach Ministry decided to have a shoe box ministry for the poor children in the area. They had applied back in the fall for a grant from a large corporation. They hoped it would have been there before then, but as December rolled on, the money had not yet made its appearance.

The group looked to their bank account to buy hats, gloves, crayons, socks, pencils and small toys. There were at least 25 children they knew of that would be attending the December 24th Christmas Eve party. There was $140.00 to be spread out among the 25. Pastor Ivie said to wait. "Wait on God." December 20th there was nothing. Prayers went up. December 21st there was still nothing. Rats. I confess that I had a stomach ache over it all.

On December 22nd the dam broke - the angels came through. At 10 a.m. a check for the promised $2,500.00 showed up! Dollar Tree, here they came! I was blessed to be there that day. "All hands on deck!" We wrapped packages as fast as we could.

There was another knock on the door. A local company donated a whole host of turkeys! Wow!! Cooks - man your stations! LOM served 500 hot meals on Christmas Eve. We gave out 25 presents to the children of the area. The boxes were stuffed to the gills.

One of the recipients was an 18-year-old young man. He stood there crying, holding the box tight in his hands. "Why are you crying?" we asked. He told us it was his only Christmas present.

God gave to LOM beyond our wildest dreams! This is what happens when the love of Jesus impacts humanity.

BELIEVING ABOVE ALL ELSE
Jim and Ann Carter

In the 1970s, while Jim and Ann were just getting into their stride with prayer and miracles, they were at a church gathering with about 30 other people. It was for praise and worship, then a meal together.

Well, one of the families present at the meeting had a small child who went to reach up on the table for some food. The problem was, it was a very hot dish and she knocked it over onto herself before anyone could stop her.

In an instant, the little girl was scalded with second-degree burns over most portions of her body. It all seemed to happen at once. The baby was screaming; everyone was screaming! But the Holy Spirit was with them. The parents grabbed the toddler up, and everyone surrounded them with strong prayers of healing.

Within a few minutes, the child calmed down, the blisters went down, and the red skin faded to pink. Then she wiggled out of her mother's arms and went back to playing.

I love the stories that end with "and they all lived happily ever after."
Bless God.

THE MENDING OF MITCH
Mitchell Smith

In all fairness, readers, you need to know that Mitch Smith is my publisher's ex-husband and best friend. But that does not make any of his stories any less interesting!

Mitch is 52 years old as of this writing. I asked him when he thought he came to know the Lord. He had a hard time with that question because he felt he was still coming to know the Lord!

Mitch does not think that miracles are odd. He thinks they happen all the time. In fact, they are so common place we don't even notice them. Except for these following . . .

Mitch Smith surveying our land in Indiana 2012

Mitch and Mary Smith (HCAP editor) observing a beautiful sunset

ST. JOSEPH
Mitchell Smith

When Mitch was in the eighth grade, in 1972, he got sick, real sick. He had Glomerulonephritis. He went into Renal Failure, a bad place to be for an eighth grader. Mitch stated back in 1972, compared to today's medicine, all they had was witchcraft!

The doctors could tell he was really sick. At the time they couldn't do much about it. He was in the hospital and not allowed to move around in his bed or get up. He needed kidney dialysis. Mitch was on the schedule to go down and have the procedure when a little old retired nun popped her head in the door. She visited kids who were in dire straits.

She started to talk to him when she realized Mitch was too sick to respond. She said to him, "Don't worry. Saint Joseph is going to take care of his boy."

That night, Mitch told his nurse he needed to go urinate. They brought him the urinal. Normally he would pass an ounce of urine that looked like a dark cola. It was so concentrated and strong it would burn as it passed through.

But this night, he passed close to a liter of normal urine, without dialysis, thank you!

Every half hour to 45 minutes, his body passed normal urine with no pain. He got very little sleep that first night. He weighed 160 pounds with all the held water, and in two days he was back down to the normal weight of a 13-year-old boy. He still has stretch marks from this event.

DADDY

Later in life, Mitch was diagnosed as infertile. He would not be able to be a daddy. It was a horrible diagnosis, and the tests hurt!

23

While in the Army, Mitch was assigned as a peace keeper for the Camp David Accords in the Sinai Desert. They were stationed in what is now a booming little resort town. But back then it was just another place in the desert. For R & R, (rest and recuperation), the Army sent them to Mt. St. Katrina's Monastery in Mt. Sinai. They were glad to go because even a Monastery was entertaining compared to a spot in the desert!

Mitch spoke with one of the Greek monks. There were no Catholic chaplains for their task force at that time. The monk asked him if he had any children.

Mitch replied, "No."

"Why not?"

"I can't." He went on to explain what the doctors had told him.

Miracle words came forth from the monk's mouth. "I want you to go over to that well and get a drink of water. I am going to go get you a medal."

Mitch went over to the well and did as he was instructed. Then he walked back over to the monk. The monk was giggling.

Mitch's first thought was, "I'm an American. What's wrong with the water?" There were a lot of the men that were suffering with Dysentery.

The monk replied, "We refuse to drink from that well. Any man who drinks from that well will father twins."

"Oh, really?"

Mitch came home on leave. His wife, Mary Dow, did indeed get pregnant. They went for the sonogram and it was twins!

There it was! Glory!
What a miracle to go from infertile to fathering twins.
Praise Ye the Lord!!

ADVERSARY
Deborah Aubrey-Peyron

Back in the winter of 2011, in early January, a dangerous flu was going around. One of the men from our church came down with it, and he came to church to be prayed over. He was running a 101-degree temperature. Mark and I went over and laid hands on him and prayed for his healing victory. I knew he was in a great battle. Bill had been sick for almost a week. He sat behind us during the service, still having trouble with a cough and breathing. I could feel the invading pathogen trying to stir up trouble in our breathing space! I prayed for understanding on how a powerful man of God could get so sick so quickly. That night, understanding came in the form of a dream.

In the dream, I was walking out of my bedroom into the living room. I saw small dark figures flying through the house. I knew they were foreign invaders of the dark kind. I started throwing the name of Jesus at them.

"In the name of Jesus," I cried over and over. I cried out, "In the name of Jesus, be gone!" They disappeared in a puff of smoke.

There, standing at the last, was the figure of a man. He had dark hair and dark eyes. He had on a suit with a black overcoat. He was not ugly in appearance. This world would have called him handsome. But what was in him was ugly. I knew he was my real adversary, God's adversary. I stopped in motion. He turned and looked up at me. I told him to leave in Jesus' name.

He just stood there staring at me.

I knew it meant trouble.

The next morning, I awoke and felt poorly. The battle for my life had just begun. By mid-afternoon, my temperature climbed higher. I called out for prayer. Our son Andy came over and prayed with Mark for my healing. I felt a little better. My temperature dipped from 102.6 to 101.6 in a matter of minutes. It was to be a short-lived victory.

The battle was in full force through the night. I was not used to being sick. I had not been really sick in years. I felt miserable. The inside of my lungs ached, and I ached all over. Mark took a couple of days off work to help me. In the course of eight weeks, we spent over $800.00 on doctor and medicine bills.

Our pastor's wife couldn't understand why I wasn't beating this. What was my problem? She thought I had "walked farther" than this in my faith. Pastor Fred prayed over me countless times. He told me to stand firm. Do not listen to the flesh!

After more than eight weeks of being ill, I had coughed so long and so hard, the tympanic membrane in my ears had moved, causing extreme vertigo to set in. I was filling up a plastic pan with vomit over and over.

Mark started to attack me. He said, "What's wrong with you? Why should I have to put up with this?"

The devil was even using my own husband against me. I felt like I was losing every battle.

One evening, friends came over and prayed with me long into the evening. I vomited up white froth. I felt it was a sign of the attack going on within me. At that time, another friend took me to see our pastor again. I asked him simply, "I will win this battle?"

He shook his head yes. Ever so gently he said, "You will win this. Every day you will get better."

I knew he saw my healing.

But I was still throwing up. By the third day of the ninth week, Mark took me back to the doctor. She gave me medicine to stop the vomiting and coughing, so my body could heal and rest. I *badly* needed rest.

Later that day, Mark's intolerance of sick people came to a head in our marriage. Before the medicine could start working, in a plastic pan on the kitchen floor, I was sick again. Mark was in the bathroom when I called out for him. Under his breath, he made cruel remarks about me. I thought at first I had heard him wrong. I got up off the floor and went to ask him what he said. The expression on his face told all I needed to know.

I went to the bedroom and got my pillow and blanket. I went to stay in the back bedroom and prayed for God's help. There was more than one battle going on; the battle for my health and the battle over my husband's hard heart.

I was exhausted and spent. I had no energy to take on an uncaring husband. I cried out to the Lord, "I'm done! I'm through. Either You put kindness and apology in his heart, or tomorrow morning, I'm leaving for my mother's home!" I was in a state.

After an hour and a half, Mark came to where I was laying down and apologized. He asked me to come to bed. I told him I would but we were talking everything out.

Mark laid down in our bed and put his arms out for me. I sat across the bed. It was time for all the victories to come in. I started the conversation, "Why do you treat me so badly when I am sick? Why won't you help me?"

He replied, "It's not just you, it's anyone. I don't like to be around sick people."

I brought up another point, "I help you when you are sick."

Mark again replied, "I don't ask you to help me. You do it because you want to. I don't want to."

There it was; his lack of compassion for people. A big road block was in the way of his heart, and with the help of the Holy Spirit, I was going to move it! With determination, I set wisdom and understanding in motion. I said, "Listen to me! You want people to think what a good, godly man you are.

27

But you aren't. Inside yourself, you despise sick people. That isn't Christ-like. When sick people came to Jesus, He had compassion on them. He healed them. He took care of them. Jesus is my example for what I do to help people. This is me. This is not you. You are not Christ-like in this, which means you have a spirit on you of an anti-Christ! Do you understand all of this?"

Understanding spread over Mark in an instant. His eyes widened with the new revelation in his spirit. Then he cried. Healing came. Mark apologized to me and to God. The powerful spirit he had on him his whole life came out and left! In an instant, his heart and soul—and our marriage-- healed. Bless God! We held each other tightly.

That very night, the spirit of illness broke over my body. I started to heal.

And bless the man. Mark took more days off from work to stay with me and help me. He bought me every different kind of Popsicle and cracker he could find, ginger-ale and soup too! He was now the kind and compassionate man I knew he could be.

He could now have the heart of Jesus.

With God, we won three important battles that week. My health was restored, the block in Mark's heart was gone, and our happy marriage was back!

The adversary was thrown out!

Alleluia!

Miraculous Interventions™ III:
2012 The Miraculous Year

Deborah Aubrey-Peyron

A diary following the year 2012's miraculous occurrences in healing, prosperity and even through sorrows.

TWINS FOUR YEARS APART!
(Jan. 17ᵗʰ)

"Momma! I have something awesome to tell you." Thomas Andrew, our youngest son had started the conversation. I was all ears.

"Do tell!"

Andy started, "I was working out at the gym today and hurt my intercostal (ribs) muscles right lateral. I had a bulge in the area. Later in the day, I called Ben to ask what to do about it. During the conversation, I mentioned I was hurting. Ben asked me if it was on my right side intercostal muscles, describing exactly what I was feeling. I was amazed and said, 'Yes.' He said he had been hurting there all day and wondered what he had done to himself. Then he asked me if my right shoulder was giving me any trouble. I said, 'Yeah,' to that. It was popping and I didn't know what I had done to it. He said it wasn't me, it was him. He had hurt his shoulder. We were feeling each other's pain. Then he asked me if I ever felt like I was his twin. (Ben had a twin that had passed away at 12 weeks gestational age.) I said, 'Yeah,' and he said, 'Me too!'"

Andy asked me, "Do you think this is possible?"

My reply? "With God, all things are possible. Absolutely! Remember when Ben was having his cardiac event in the army? You came home and knew there was something wrong with him."

Andy replied, "Yeah, just like a twin four years apart."

This does not surprise me one bit. God answers the prayers of a child.

When Ben was very young, he missed his twin and used to pray for God to send him back.

A PROPHET'S MANTLE
(April 10th)

This day was set aside as a day of help for our pastor and his wife, Fred and Jeanne Schuppert. Mark did all their yard work—which was formidable—and I made them dinner. I even made them an Easter basket with only Christ-themed candy in it!

I arrived to find a busy household. Mark was still diligently working in the yard, and Jeanne was teaching music as I brought in their afternoon meal. I had just set it all on the kitchen counter when Pastor Fred walked in. He looked tired and weak but happy to see me. I showed him what I brought for their dinner and their Easter basket. Fred chuckled over receiving an Easter basket at the ripe old age of 64. It figured it would come from me! I asked if I could talk with him for a few minutes, and he nodded yes and sat down to listen.

I had a vision back in the middle of March. I was taken out of my body and shown God's will for our pastor's life— what was to be. I knew the time to share had come. I started the conversation.

"Fred, you know how you've told us to talk to God as a friend, and He will answer us?"

"Yes, that's right."

"Well, I did that back in early March. I asked the Lord a simple question. I said, 'Lord, what are we going to do about Fred?' Immediately, I was not in my body or on my couch anymore. I have only had a handful of visions in my life and only when they are important. When they happen, I try to pay close attention."

"Yes, yes, go on."

"I saw you standing in front of me. You had on a prophet's mantle. It was white. You looked strong and determined. You turned to the side, and there was another

31

man standing there. I think it was your oldest son. You took off your mantle and put it on him. Then, you turned back toward me, looked at me one last time, and then turned and walked away. I knew I would never see you again on this Earth. Immediately, I was back on my couch. The only thing I am not sure of is this; if you are going back to Illinois or going home."

Fred was quiet for a moment, then he spoke up, "I have been waiting for someone to come and tell me this."

I thanked God I had been given a chance to speak the prophetic word. I thanked Fred for his ministry and told him that we loved him very much. He said he loved us too. And, just like in the prophesy, Fred gave his mantle to his oldest son, and I never saw him alive again after that.

I'M ALIVE!
(May 15th)

I awoke with a great start! My heart pounded in my chest! My eyes were wide open, and alert. I sat straight up in bed at the sound of the familiar voice as it shouted with awe.

"I'm alive!"

I knew without a doubt, our pastor had just moved from our three-dimensional world to a world with no limitations. Fred had gone to a world that he was so fond of saying, "under the spout where the glory pours out!"

That same morning, I heard from Pastor Ivie Dennis. Ivie called to tell me she had seen it all happen in her spirit. She saw Fred pass from this life to the next.

Of course she had!

Later that day, the news was verified by different church members that called our house. But Ivie and I, already knew.

It was time to go to work. I called friends for provisions to send for his family that would come back to our area.

A local church was most gracious to hold services and agreed to supply a good portion of the meal.

"AND THE FATHER LOVES HIS SON"
The Book of Matthew

John 3:16 *"For God so loved the World that*
He gave His only begotten Son,
that whosoever believeth in Him,
should not perish, but have everlasting life."

There once was a little boy with bright blue inquisitive eyes, and strawberry-blonde hair that stood straight up on his head! No amount of coaxing with either water, gel or spit, could tame this young'uns hair—or spirit. His name was Matthew.

Now Matthew came into our lives as part of a part-and-parcel with his sister, Lily. Their mother, Samantha, and our youngest son, Thomas Andrew, had fallen in love.

We met the family in Samantha's front yard. We had been heading back home from Mom Peyron's, and Andy was behind us in a pickup truck. He beeped his horn for us to let him in front. Then, Andy motioned for us to follow him. Miss Samantha had just gotten off work from the emergency room, and Andy thought it was as good a time as any for us to say our hellos.

As the four of us introduced ourselves, two small children peeked their heads out the front window. Before we knew it, they came running out of the house. One skipped over to us, Miss Lily, and the other, Matthew, ran like the wind—possibly tornadic, as he did circles around and around everyone!

"Matthew!" Heads turned to follow his progress.

"Matthew!!" Dizziness began to set in.

"Matthew!"

Over the course of the next year, I was occasionally called on to babysit as the two adults became a couple. We have shared many interesting meals together. Both children knew about prayer and Jesus. Samantha's childhood household was half-Catholic and half-Protestant. When we made the sign of the cross before and after meals and at bedtime, it was somewhat familiar to her children.

Lily asked why we made the sign of the cross, and I shared with her the best understanding I had to give to a six-year-old.

"It's like opening up a conversation. Instead of just diving in to what you plan to say, it's rather like an introduction. For example, 'Hello, Lord, I'm starting my prayer. Lord God, Jesus my Savior, and the Holy Spirit please be in attendance.'

'In the name of the Father, and of the Son, and of the Holy Spirit... in their names, I lift up these prayers.'"

It made good-enough sense to Lily. Pretty soon, she was making the sign of the cross with us at meals, whenever we would hear a siren—as a silent prayer to go out to whoever needed it at the time, or when someone wasn't feeling well. She would plant the sign of the cross with her fingers, squarely on the ill person's forehead.

But Matthew saw and heard these actions differently than we did. After we would all pray at the end and say our closure, Matthew would say it too, or so I thought.

One evening, while I was having dinner with Andy, Sam and the kids, after our prayer, conversation started.

Samantha said, "Momma?"

I replied, "Yes, Dear?"

"Have you ever heard Matthew pray at the end of prayers as you make the sign of the cross?"

"Yes, I think so." I sought my memories to give me a clue.

Samantha turned toward her son and smiled sweetly, "Mattie, what do you say at the end of a prayer?"

Matthew smiled and said something shyly that I didn't quite catch. I looked at Sam with a question. Samantha smiled and repeated Matthew's rendition.

"He said, 'and the Father loves His Son,'" as she made the sign of the cross.

Revelation hit me like a solid rock! This precious little tornado had understood far better than many a gray-haired theologian had ever taught!

"And the Father Loves His Son."
This is the word of the Lord.
Thanks be to God.

John 3:17 *"For God sent not His Son into the world to condemn the world; but that the world through Him might be saved."*

Miraculous Interventions™ IV
The Gathering Season

Deborah Aubrey-Peyron

People from hundreds of miles away were called to a little town in Southern Indiana. While the secular world forced division and separation, the Holy Spirit gathered His people for signs, healings and preparation for what is to come.

THE PAPER CROSS
(The first week of December, 2014)

Gifts from the heart can take many forms; but they most always emit an emotional response from the receiver. Be blessed with what you have and your loved ones that surround you.

It had been a rough couple of years for Mark and me. Over the last six years, I had lost my job, we had to sell our land, we were without a home of our own for a whole year, and my mother had passed away. At the end of all that havoc, Mark and I finally settled down into a nice little suburban home in Corydon, Indiana. It was just in time for other's needs to show up at our new front door....

SUMMER OF 2014

I had just unpacked the last moving box when calls started coming in...

"Yes, son...of course we can help keep your children through the summer. I have a request. You live so far away, on the days you want us to keep Matt and Lily in succession, may they stay with us instead of us driving back and forth between houses? It would help us with the gas cost. We're a little tight, money-wise, right now."

Lily and Matthew ended up with us four days a week all summer long.

At the same time, our friend Lisa was getting ready to go through a messy divorce. Due to a dream given to me weeks before, I felt her request coming. I spoke with Mark about her predicament. He asked me where we would put five more people along with Matt and Lily. I told him God knew.

By the first week of June, the call came. They, like us the year before, were about to be homeless.

Lisa said, "He laid hands on me. He hurt me." She sounded so sad.

I replied, "Come on. You can't stay there any longer. We'll make it somehow. Come on."

Mark came home that evening to a household of nine.

We'd already put all the money we managed to save into our new home. And the garden we planted had only been in for a few weeks. There was not enough food in our home or budget to feed nine people a day.

The first week of June, on a bright sunny morning, I went out to our garden alone for a talk. I sat. Speaking to the garden, I said, "Okay, listen. Here's the deal. We have nine people in our home that we can't feed. You have to come up quickly and feed us. I will come out every morning and pray over you. I'll even sing praise songs. I will feed and water you. But I need you to keep your end of the deal."

In the meantime, friends gathered around and gave money and groceries to the "cause" -- 'cause we didn't have any, yet.

All the timing went perfectly.

By the end of June, just three short weeks after my first prayer, we had food-a-plenty out of our garden. Tomatoes, squash, green peppers, green beans and more were at the ready. It looked like a feast to us!

In the late summer, another friend found Lisa and her children a home, for the time being, not too far from us. During the fall, we still had many meals together. Later, it was decided that Lisa and her four children would move to Texas to be with her parents, to have family support.

As Thanksgiving approached, Lisa said they would stay long enough for one more celebration together. It was agreed the kids would trim our downstairs' Christmas tree. Lisa's children were very thoughtful and kind, especially considering all that they had been through in those last months. Lisa has two older children and two younger children.

We set up for one last Sunday meal together. They arrived on time. I made one of their favorite meals; homemade chicken pot pie. Greetings were given, prayers were said and conversation commenced. Lisa spoke about the coming move and all it would entail. The younger children were excited about decorating our Christmas tree, eating homemade cookies . . . and opening presents!

After dinner, while the adults were cleaning up the kitchen, the younger children went downstairs to draw and color while waiting for us to bring in the boxes for tree-trimming. After a bit, young Adam came upstairs.

"Mrs. Peyron, may I have a piece of tape?" he asked.

"Sure, I'll get it for you." I handed him a piece.

Adam went back downstairs. We joined them a few minutes later.

While the children were putting ornaments on the tree, Adam came up to me with something in his hand. He stood shyly before me and spoke softly.

"Mrs. Peyron, I didn't have any money to get you something for Christmas, so I made you something."

From behind his back, Adam brought out his present; two torn slips of paper taped together in the form of a cross.

I studied his small token of affection for a minute. I understood the love it represented—just like the love given 2,000 years ago; born in a stable and died on a wooden cross—and the lack in Adam's meager household.

Fighting back tears, I smiled. "Come upstairs Adam. I know the perfect place for it."

We walked up the stairs together and into our living room where the children's Christmas tree stood. The paper cross had nothing to attach itself to the tree, so I laid it on a branch over the nativity set.

"Adam, as long as there is breath in my body, your gift will be placed on the children's tree over our nativity every year in remembrance of this day."

Adam nodded his head soberly then went back downstairs with the other children. I sat with tears running down my face as I pondered my special gift from a homeless child. It will be with me always.

DROWNING
(After Christmas)

Crystal Murray had come over for a day of editing. While there, we stopped for a bite of lunch. As usual, I multitasked. I got out my calendar and we set up for that night and the rest of the week together.

I commented, "I can only watch part of the show tonight. You tell me about what I miss."

Crystal inquired, "Why? Are you busy in the middle of the program?"

"No," I replied. "I can't watch someone possibly drown. It upsets me. I can't breathe—I panic inside."

My little sister—sent to me by Christ Jesus to make my world more complete—got quiet. She sought an answer from the Holy Spirit. Something was amiss with her big sister. What could it be? Then in the Spirit, Crystal heard, *"She drowned in the womb."*

"Oh, Deb! I know what's wrong. You drowned in your mother's womb..."

The room went quiet with revelation. I stopped in my tracks.

Quickly my memory went back to what I had been told all of my life. I was born very premature—eleven weeks early with both lungs collapsed and was blue by my third day. My momma was told I wouldn't make it. She refused to accept it. Instead, Momma claimed, "This baby will live and not die."

But Crystal was right.

I had drowned.

I had died.

My heart raced.

Her statements loomed over me.

Not only had my mother and God been in agreement as to my outcome, but my first miracle was not at three-days-old as I had always believed, but sooner. Before I had ever left my mother's womb, I was raised from the dead. My second miracle was at three days old.

It was just like Lisa Horn had told me three years earlier while at Believer's Fellowship, "The devil tried to kill you before you were born. *Before…*"

I was speechless. The implication was staggering.

What do I do now?

Whatever God tells me to do.

And keep writing…

THE OPEN WINDOW
(January 15, 2015)

Sometimes warnings are given in dreams and it is best to heed them.

I woke up with my heart pounding in my chest. I'd had a bad dream. Someone I knew had gotten into our home through an open window. I could still see, in my mind's eye, the shadowy figure stalking through our home.

In the dream, Mark had a shotgun in his hands and went looking for the elusive figure bent on harming us—harming me…

Mark felt me stir and woke up.

"Honey, are you okay?"

"I had a bad dream. A bad, bad dream." I was still panting.

"It's okay now, honey." Mark said as he tried to comfort me.

"No, no. I need you to check every window in the house."

"Why, what happened in your dream?" By then Mark was up on his elbow and looking at me with concern.

"I think someone broke in through an open window. In my dream, the window in the spare bedroom was unlocked. Someone was in the house."

Exasperated that he had to get out of bed, Mark flung off the covers and said, "Honey, we don't have any unlocked windows in this house! But I'll check the spare bedroom just to make you happy."

"Thank you," I mumbled.

Mark went around the corner and into the other bedroom and checked the window. He climbed up on the bed and tried the window. It opened with ease. Someone had unlocked it…

Mark shut the window back and locked it. He asked me from there, "Honey did you unlock this window lately?"

"NO!" I shouted.

Mark came stomping back into our bedroom. He had a determined look on his face.

"Stay here!" He commanded.

Mark grabbed his shotgun, took off the safety, and just like in the dream, he searched our house. He started with looking under our very bed. I almost threw up.

As he cleared each room, Mark called out, "Nothing" or, "Clear!"

Mark searched our first floor, the sunroom, the basement, even the garage and our front porch.

I sat in our bed with tears in my eyes, and I prayed for my husband. I waited for him to come back to bed. After a few minutes, the all-clear was given, and we huddled a little closer together as we fell into an uneasy sleep.

WHEN GOD HOLDS MY FEET TO THE FIRE
(First week of October, 2015)

It was a story on the road. A revelation while on the way to Tennessee to see my Uncle Paul and Aunt Marilyn. The Lord wanted me to see how He works in my life. This revelation was not just for me, but to help others as well. And to go on with my mission.

Mark and I were travelling through Kentucky to Tennessee to see my Uncle Paul and Aunt Marilyn. They are a precious Baptist couple and we enjoy visiting with them whenever we can. Mark was driving and I was the navigator. As has happened many times in my life, revelation came in an instant.

I saw it all happen before my eyes. My past came alive once more. Thomas Andrew, our youngest son, was being born.

Two doctors walked into the room. They were getting ready to take me back to perform a cesarean section for the birth of our third son, Thomas Andrew.

The anesthesiologist looked at my chart.

"I see this will be number three cesarean for you?"

"Yes, sir."

"This is your last baby?"

"Yes, sir."

"Have you seen any of your babies born?"

"No, sir. They were both emergency C-sections."

"Well, you are going to see this baby fresh out of the hatch."

"Oh, okay."

"Remember, we are on the same side. This is your last chance to see this miracle."

"Yes, sir."

The epidural was given and they wheeled me into the operating room. It was shortly after that, the battle began. True to what my obstetrician had told me, I did not feel the incision. But after a minute or two, I felt pressure. What they hadn't told me was I would feel them moving my pelvic bones to get the baby out.

I started screaming. Loud. "Put me under! Put me under! Pain! Pain!"

Immediately the anesthesiologist said, "What kind?"

"Pressure!" I cried. "Like my bones are moving!"

"That's right. We have to get the baby out." He was very calm. After all, it wasn't his bones they were moving.

Hollering ensued. "Oxygen! Oxygen! Under! Under!" I was hysterical.

By now, it was an all-out fight.

"No way! You are going to see this baby being born and that's it! It's your last baby!" The obstetrician rolled his eyes at the two of us and worked faster.

It was a loud argument between a woman strapped down to a gurney and the man who held her life in his hands. Once again, how smart am I?

That was when I heard Andy cry. It stopped me in my tracks. All my pain and suffering ended.

"Why is my baby crying?"

Laughter started.

"He was just born. We get them to cry to breathe."

I was finally all smiles. The mission was accomplished and both doctors sighed with relief.

"Bring me my baby!"

That command they were happy to comply with.

When they brought Andy over for me to see, his head was turned away from me. I said his name, "Hello Thomas Andrew."

Immediately he turned his head toward me and looked my way.

That was when I heard the "click, zing." I thought, "Who in their right mind has a camera in here?" It was my nurse. She caught a Polaroid picture of the first time Andy and I laid eyes on each other. And I was smiling like it was nobody's business. I cried happy tears like I was the one that had just been born. It was the best moment of my life.

You see, their sternness with me was for my own good. And I thank them to this day. And the nurse who took the picture.

The same is with God and me, as He moves me closer and through my mission field. I am sure I have kicked and screamed 70% of the way, not trusting He knows best for me. But our glorious Lord knows my form, and that I will be overjoyed as I arrive at each destiny He has for me. And that it will benefit not only me, but those around me. After all, that's what makes me happiest; sharing.

And the Great I AM also knows I will happily tell on my silly self, especially if it benefits others, too. I have no problem sharing my faults along the way of life.

You see, if I can show the progress of overcoming my fears of moving forward and God's patience with me, then maybe my readers can see their journey a little differently, too.

Bringing peace to people one reader at a time.

"Blessed are the peace makers, for they shall be called children of God."

Sermon on the Mount
Matthew 5:9

Miraculous Interventions™ V
The Small, Still Voice
An Intimate Walk with God

Deborah Aubrey-Peyron
with contribution by *David Merk*

"Come walk with me, and I will answer questions from your past. All that you have desired in your heart to understand. Sit with me a while and learn."

And so it began.

WHEN MY SON CALLS
(The afternoon of September 4)

Our son, David contacted me and said he loves me. I told him I love him too. Mark and he exchanged the same greeting of love. I asked about his life and he brought me up to date. I was very supportive and told him we would help him in any way he might need. He thanked me and wished us a good night. I love you son!

Thank you God for this large miracle of David reaching out. And David called us the next Sunday too!

When My Son Calls
The Story
Psalm 4: 3 "...The Lord will hear when I call unto Him." KJV

We have three, fine, upstanding sons with three different personalities. None better than the other, just different in the way they react or correspond with the family.

The oldest, Ben, is much like me, only better! He and I are loveable, likeable, "puppies." If you are crying, Ben or I, will cry with you. We ooze compassion.

"Hello! How are ya! I love ya! Come on, give me a hug. Do you need help with anything? When can I see you?" As busy as they are with school and work, we see this one and his wife, Amanda, as often as possible.

Andy, the youngest, also has a compassionate heart. He and his growing family like to help out at the homeless shelters by bringing laughter and smiles to the families there, in the way of movie nights. He packs up his wife, Samantha, and children, along with his equipment - plus plenty of popcorn, and the latest Disney flick, to share happy moments with people who seem to have so few of them. If you are crying, Andy will do his best to make you feel better with a smile or a new outlook. Now this boy, is busy! He works all he can to support his growing family. The child is busy making a million dollars one week at a time! We see Andy and family when he has the time to spare.

David, our middle son, is also a busy man. Not yet married like his brothers, he works and goes to school. David is our quiet child that we hear from the least. I do not believe he loves us any less, just has a quieter way of showing it.

But if that young man calls either my husband or myself, we drop everything we are doing and take his call! We eagerly wait to hear what is on his mind or heart. Why, he might even need us! When David calls, it means he is reaching out to us and we want to make sure he knows, we are reaching back.

I imagine it must be the same with our Heavenly Father. He eagerly awaits to hear from each of us, even though it may be a long time in between conversations. How overjoyed our Abba Father must be when we reopen communication with Him. I can only imagine, He too, would drop everything, even the 99*, to come and answer our call. After all, God wants us to know, when we reach out to Him, He is already reaching out to us.

*See Jesus' parable of the Good Shepherd. Matt 18:12.

51

DAVID'S TURN TO TELL A STORY

(May 8th, 2016, 8:58 p.m.)

By David Merk

Growing up in Lanesville, with two brothers and being raised by a single mom, I had no idea how poor we were.

All of our school supplies were donated.

Our groceries were donated.

Christmas was donated.

But every Sunday my brothers and I would go to church and when they were passing the basket, mom would give us, maybe a dollar or a couple of dimes to donate.

I remember one Sunday, she gave my brothers' quarters and me a nickel. I asked her if I too could have a quarter to put in the collection and I'll never forget her reply.

"Honey, that's all the money we have in the world."

Every Sunday she would give everything we had, however much or little it was, so the church could help families like ours.

We wound up moving to the Charlestown projects. She told my brothers and I to draw pictures of what we thought it would look like. Even though it was smaller and government-subsidized, she made it sound like a castle. She knew we had lost our home. She knew how poor we were, and she still gave everything she had.

Deborah Aubrey-Peyron, you are the strongest person I know. And even though I don't like it when you tag me in things or comment on my wall, I am so grateful that you were so strong for us when it would have been much easier to sell Paul or Thomas to the gypsies.

You taught me how to give with all of my heart, and because of everything you've been through I know I can make it through anything life throws at me.

You are the world's best mom. Happy Mother's Day!

Well, after I was through crying while reading his post the first time, I replied to him on Facebook, "David Merk, you really noticed. Thank you son. You and your brothers (the ones I didn't sell to the gypsies) have made me very proud. I love you, Momma."

David replied shortly after that with, "I forgot to say this up there but I love you too, Momma."

DON'T FORGET
(Mid-Feb.)

Do you wonder if you are really making a difference for the Kingdom of God? Watch your enemies....that'll tell you.

Around the middle of February, Mark and I were shopping at a national store in New Albany. I was looking in a bin, (possibly towels as I remember) when another lady walked up and looked in the bin too. She was very ordinary looking. Short dark hair, dressed casually, middle-class. I thought she was fine until she opened her mouth and started to speak.

She said quietly, "So when is the exact date that Jesus is coming back?"

Before I could form a thought, I spoke clearly out of my spirit, "I would be a liar if I told you I knew the exact date Jesus was coming back!"

Immediately my armor was on. My face was set and my eyes were sharp. I was not friendly.

She looked from side to side with her eyes rolled upward in a sly motion. Curtly once, she nodded her head, and put down what she was looking at. She left quickly. The unwelcome visitor went in one direction and I went in the other. I headed straight for my husband!

What does this tell us? The devil knows that time is short. And he can tell who is walking close with the Lord and watching the times we are living in.

I wondered, could he see the light of God and the Blood of Jesus on me? After all, I am a scribe. Now, not only for miracles, signs and wonders, but as a watcher for the times we are living in.

Everyone – look for Jesus, point to Jesus. He is coming back!

OUT OF MY BODY
(Mid-Feb.)

It had been almost 20 years since I had been taken out of my body and seen from space the happenings on the Earth. I thought that time was over in my life. After all, it had been so long...

I was once again taken out in space. I had no fear, no gasping. It was very ordinary to me. I was sure I was with my angel.

I turned and looked toward the Earth. I saw our planet, and not far off from it, I saw a red, larger planet heading straight for the earth. I knew it meant sudden destruction.

I started screaming for all I was worth, "Stay Your hand, Lord! Stay Your hand!" As the planet moved closer and closer, I continued to yell, "Lord, please, stay Your hand!!"

I had sheer panic for the inhabitants of the Earth.

It ended as quickly as it came.

Miraculous Interventions™ VI
Warn Those Who Will Listen

Deborah Aubrey-Peyron

Specific prophesied warnings had come "down the pipe" regarding a nuclear attack on American soil. This is the story of the struggle to tell all the right people, that it would get to the highest ranking in order for them to find it and stop it in time.

THE DEATH OF THE SOUL

My introduction to the Book of Revelation was at 24 years old. At the time, I was married to an unsaved man who was never around. He was a rounder, if you know what I mean. But I was a good, little Roman Catholic girl—and stayed married for a long season.

On lonely evenings, I would look up scripture chapters that I hadn't read yet. One night, I stumbled onto the Book of Revelation. As I got almost half-way through it, an unusual sleep fell over me.

I had this dream:

I could see myself lying on my bed still reading the Book of Revelation. I looked down in my dream and saw the words on the page. I had no idea which chapter it was—and was never able to find it again. But the words that I saw are still with me to this day.

"The first death is the death of the body. The second death to fear, is the death of the soul. (The one that is not prescribed to heaven.)

I really believe hell and the lake of fire are intended for the devil, his fallen angels and their offspring—those that follow satan. Yes, I believe—just like the Bible teaches in Genesis—the fallen angels took wives, bore children, and we fight their offspring and remnant to this day.

You may ask, but what about Noah's flood? Didn't it kill all life on the planet but Noah and his family? All over the ruination of the original seed God had planted.

Let's talk about that.

The angelic beings were eternal beings—they couldn't be killed. Only their offspring could die. Unfortunately what that meant, they could start over again too...

Any evidence of that? The mighty men of old and renown in this day and age to support my hypothesis?

Yes. In the last war in Afghanistan. Have you not heard of the Giant of Kandahar? The monstrosity of a man who was well over 15 feet tall. It came out of an Afghanistan cave wielding a seven-foot spear. It killed one of our men. And it took a platoon of men shooting it directly in the face to take it down and kill it.

...And they say there were more...

Evil exists. Just as I was told when I was 44 years old, sitting at my work desk. A witch—cackle included—called me for help with a prescription. As she was cackling on the phone in my left ear, in my right ear, I heard an angel speak.

"Hang up the phone. You are speaking to the damned. Hang up the phone! You are still speaking to the damned!"

I hung up quickly.

So, if there are damned on the earth, from lucifer, headed for the lake of fire, it makes great sense that there are saved people on this earth. Saints prescribed for Heaven. Right?

And just maybe, those in the middle, after the Great White Throne judgement, qualify for what I saw. The death of the soul. They belong to neither place. Could it be?

THE CHICAGO STORY
(2014)

It was another lovely Sunday afternoon at the Becker's in Lexington, Kentucky. I was still working on building David's book trying to put 74 years' worth of experiences and travels into one book. I was pretty sure I was outnumbered from the very beginning.

As David started telling his next story, I realized it was not for his book. He was telling me what had just occurred and I needed to listen. It was important.

David said, "Deborah, the Holy Spirit told me America is going to be attacked."

I looked up from my writing. Concerned, I asked, "Oh? How?"

David replied, "By a nuclear bomb in Chicago."

I dropped my pen and listened with mounting fear.

He went on.

"It will come from up in the Canadian waters. Down through the St. Lawrence River and the Michigan Lakes. The boat will port in the Chicago harbor and off-load the bomb on land to detonate."

I gulped.

I barely asked, "Did the Holy Spirit tell you when?"

David shook his head no.

I replied very soberly, "Well, if you don't mind, I'm not telling this story in full until I get verification. Then I'll tell everybody."

I added a minute later, "And I hope I never get verification!"

Well, my hope held out for three short years....

AN EARLY MORNING HOUR
(End of June, 2017)

I could see we were still on vacation in Walt Disney World. We were staying in a nice room. We were having tea on the breakfast bar. I looked down on the counter and saw a calendar with the date of September 30 highlighted.

In my dream, I argued with the Lord. I said in my head, "Lord, we aren't going to be in Walt Disney World on September 30th. We are supposed to check out by the 28th."

At that instant, a tall, black lady in a blue-stripe dress came walking in. She had a small package in her hand. She chuckled to herself and said to me, "I brought you a package for your birthday."

She left the room quickly. Mark and I looked at each other and he asked me, "Do you know her?"

I replied, "She looks familiar..."

As soon as she had left our room, a tall, thin black man walked in. He was full of self-importance and haughtiness. He too carried a small package. He walked over and put it on the counter. He also said, "I have a package for your birthday." We stared after him as he left. Mark and I looked at each other with perplexity.

I asked Mark to look and see if they were still outside. I didn't want their packages. Mark went to the living room window and opened the curtains. They were sitting in chairs on the porch. We could hear them talking.

She said, "She's so stupid."

He replied, "I wonder if they recognize it's us, yet?"

By then, boy was I mad! I was shouting as I was putting on my shoes to take them back their packages.

I grabbed the two packages, and started out the front door. As I opened the door and walked out, I heard him laughing.

He said, "I'm not through with America yet...."

Sidebar: Two days later, Sam called me and said she and Andy had been talking. They felt we were supposed to stay in the WDW hotel through the 30th of September. When I told Mark what she said without knowing anything, he replied, "Make it so."

And I did.

CONFIRMATION OF MY DREAM

Two days after I had my dream about the packages, I heard on Facebook, (sure not from national news), N. Korea fired a missile and sent a message to President Trump.

He sent, "I'm sending a package for your birthday." (Meaning July 4th.)

It was almost the exact same words from my dream, a couple nights before. Ominous to be sure. From the first week of July through the middle of August, the North Korean leader, threatened America and her allies with nuclear attacks. This was the backdrop to our whole unfolding story.

Mark and I fasted and prayed for days against the schemes of the enemy.

God help us. Oh, God help us!

THE PS INCIDENT
(Third week of July, 2017)

On the heels of the prophecy, we were supposed to go to a Pastor's conference in Louisville, Kentucky. Now this was a well-known young man with great words of knowledge and study. We were always pleased to hear him speak.

The first evening Mark and I, Katie and Nick went together. Boy did we have fun! The pulpit was on fire with words from the Lord and singing with the choirs.

The next morning, Katie and I went by ourselves. Mark and Nick had to work. I told Katie while on the way there, I felt compelled to tell the pastor's first-in-command. But at the time, I had no idea how far up the ladder this message would go. And who would eventually bring me revelation my important message reached its destination.

Katie and I arrived just in time for the start of the morning conference. All the seats in the middle were taken. We either had to sit on the left or right. It was a 50/50 choice. We chose the seats on the left.

Before pastor started his opening sentences, he stopped. He walked over to our side of the room, pointed in our direction, and said, "Someone over here has had a very important dream. You have to write it down."

Katie and I looked at each other, feeling his words were intended for us. For me.

An hour-and-a-half went quickly by as the morning came to a close. Once more, pastor came back to our side, pointed, and said, "By the way,

I'm going to see the president next week."

I dropped my jaw and looked at Katie. The Lord had told me in my Spirit—not a couple of days before—our story would get before the President of the United States. At the time I had practically shouted that I had no idea how that would happen!

We hurriedly got up to find pastor's right-hand man. We asked to speak to him privately. He nodded his head and we went to the church kitchen. I stammered through the first couple of sentences. Katie took up the next part of the story and I took over mid-way. We told him about all the confirmations and my latest dream with the date. We told him about North Korea.

As he was walking out, Katie asked, "Do you get warnings from people much?"

He turned to face us and said, "Yes, but not like this, with this much detail and not about North Korea. Can you type this up and have it to me by tonight?"

I replied, "Yes, sir. I sure can."

I paused for a second and said, "Listen, I didn't put any stock into Y2K, and I wasn't a bit worried about December 2012."

He questioned me, "and the eclipse?"

I said, "Be serious! It's just an eclipse! I'm being serious!"

He nodded his head, evidently it was the correct answer.

I went on, "But this, from the time I found out about it three years ago, it hasn't left me. And when it was confirmed, well, my tummy aches over it... Please do something."

He nodded his head and went out the door.

Miraculous Interventions™ VII
The Saving of America

Deborah Aubrey-Peyron

In the previous book, a dire warning had gone out. Had I told all of the right people? Was there real proof of the warning we had been given in the Spirit? How did the autumn of 2017 unfold? This is the rest of the story.

DREAMING IN DISNEY
(September 28, 2017)
(5:30 a.m.)

After a nice meal and walk around together, the kids went home to pack for their weekend with us. And we went back to our resort to rest for the busy weekend ahead. Even as urgent as the message had been that had brought us there, I went to sleep at ease, to finally rest...

My "Telling" Time

I went to sleep and opened my eyes. I saw hell. It was all around me. I was in hell but not a part of it. It was as if I was falling down a long, black hole, deep into the earth. I saw what I thought was coal glistening and flash firing in the walls of the cavern as I fell endlessly downward. I soon found I was being directed where to go.

In this vision/dream, I reached a large cavern, bigger than I could take all in. I did not stop there. There was a second cave, farther down into the depths of hell, off to the side. As if it had been dug deeper into the very pit of hell. I was aware of a stench, horrors, sorrow and despair; but they were not a part of me nor of my experience.

I realized I was with an angel and it brought me great comfort. We slowed our progress and came to a room lit by a single candle. There was a table with no chairs—for there is no comfort in hell.

On the table were plans of a sort. Much like you would see in a situation war room. Out of the darkness to gather around the table, came hideous demons dressed in general's uniforms. The most ugly of all—ha' satan—lucifer himself— walked up to the table and spoke.

"Get ready. I am starting the war soon." His raspy voice seethed with venom giving me chills up and down my spine.

As soon as he spoke, I was back in our bedroom wide awake, heart pounding.

Immediately I was given revelation. I felt in my Spirit, "Imminent! Days! Weeks!" And I felt I knew why. The devil was trying to start a war before the second coming of Jesus Christ. Satan thought the body of Christ couldn't stop his plans without the Man-Jesus physically on the earth. Satan was once again trying to usurp God.

I gasped. "What do you want me to do?!"

In my Spirit, the reply came quick. ***"Pray the Lord's Prayer! God's will. For the devil can't win against God's will!"***

I shook my husband awake.

"Mark! Get up! I've seen hell! Been to hell! I've heard the devil's plans! We have to pray! Get your Bible please!"

The urgency in my voice got Mark's attention. He quickly grabbed his Bible and we went to Ephesians 6:10-16 - the armor of God, as a sword and a shield.

Sundown of that very day, was Yom Kippur - the Day of Atonement. I believed it.

I found out later, Katie Yocum was also up at 5:30 that morning praying. Sleep finally came back to her at 6:30. Birds of a feather prayed together 900 miles apart!

I WARNED THOSE WHO
WOULD LISTEN
A brief recap

Ever since the first warning--almost four years earlier, from Pastor David Becker in Lexington, Kentucky, of a possible nuclear strike from a rouge nation on American soil, I had an eerie feeling about his prophecy. I promised Dave that until I received verification of his prophecy, I would tell no one. But if the day ever came that I indeed verified his word of knowledge, I would tell everyone who would listen to me.

Verification came the spring of 2017, at a seminar in Louisville, Kentucky from a visiting couple from Rochester, New York. Their names were John and Carol Leary. As Carol and I confirmed the same prophecy from two different people, we knew our lives had just been joined together for a greater cause than ourselves.

I told my doctor, our local law enforcement officials, and I shared my information with local pastors and national pastors. All from May through September of 2017. And we prayed— hard— that I had done everything God expected of me. That I had gotten it all right. And I dreamed, boy did I dream.

A NUCLEAR VISION
(August 5th, 2017)

[Taken mostly, from book:
*Miraculous Interventions VI,
Warn Those Who Will Listen*]

"It was early in the morning. I am still not sure if this was indeed a vision or a dream; it came out of a mist. I could see Mark and me sleeping in bed together—peacefully sleeping.

Through closed eyes, I saw an instantaneous brilliant flash of light—it was gone in an eighth of a second—like lightening. My heart sank and I cried as I waited for the percussion of the nuclear blast to hit.

In this vision, I turned toward the clock, it was 8:15 a.m.

I realized then, I was actually turned the other way in bed—opposite of the way I saw me in the vision. When I turned over, I saw it was 7:45 a.m. But just like in the vision, I was crying.

Mark and I prayed against nuclear war from that day on—especially against the rouge country of North Korea."

I hoped and prayed God would send me a sign that my message got to all those it was sent to—especially the letter I sent to a pastor who had a date at the White House. Toward the end of August, at a church service, a word of knowledge came down the pipe from a visiting pastor.

As Apostle Larry was finishing his service, he stopped, then paced back and forth at the front of the altar.

He said, "There is someone here who had a message. And a person of influence is going to a person of great influence with your message. They will remember you. Just like the butler remembered Joseph to Potiphar, you will be remembered too."

He asked who this message was for, because God told him that person would need prayer! I raised my hand and he came running and prayed over me and for all who were around us.

I was also hopeful, later that fall, when Mark and I went on vacation, while in Tennessee, I would get a second confirmation.

Unfortunately, through less-than-crummy circumstances, Mark came down terribly ill the day we were supposed to arrive in Tennessee. We stayed in our hotel room for four days waiting to see if we could meet with the ones who held the final clue. The only thing we confirmed while there was I could get just as sick as Mark did. We had a heck of a time making it back to Indiana.

A FINAL CONFIRMATION
(Long after I thought
I had finished this book!)

While Mary and I were editing this book, and I was waiting for page reviews to come back from New York, a package arrived.

In it was a copy of a declassified report to, well, one of those "alphabet agencies," which I will not name. It was regarding the likelihood of an EMP threat from the North during the fall of 2017. And it was dated during the period of time which we were all getting alerts from heaven, to pray like crazy against an attack! Even the date of September 30th was mentioned, just like in my dream!

This was the same month that North Korea detonated an H-Bomb under their mountain. (It caused a 6.0 earthquake, reportedly bringing down internal parts of the mountain, trapping and killing a hundred people.) And it released radioactive fallout over their area.

There was much more in this declassified report that was way beyond my ability to explain here. Suffice it to say - we got it right. The threats had been real and the warning came just in time.

Prayer and obedience do matter.

GREAT AUNT KATE!
(End of November, 2017)

"Come on Katie!" I cried. "We're going out to dinner with our kids. We'll be back in time for Nick to pick you up."

"Well, I guess I could go," Katie reasoned.

"Awe, come on! You can play with baby Edward! He is so much fun!"

"Well, if you're going to play the 'baby' card, I'll go."

We met Ben, Amanda and baby at Cracker Barrel. We all sat down to a good meal. Chatter rang throughout the busy pre-Christmas atmosphere. And that's when Katie got to shine. While busily talking at our end of the table, we heard from the other end, baby laughter. Real squeals! Loud and long laughter rang out to be heard in all the building. We looked down to see a thoroughly engaged Katie Yocum giving "knucks" to our 16-month-old grandson. Edward squealed and laughed to everyone's delight.

Katie laughed right along with him. She cried out, "Knucks, Edward!"

Edward held out his baby hand in a fist. Katie put her big hand next to his and made a blow up, fizzle sound and animation with her hand. Edward squealed with delight. The harder he laughed, the more it became contagious. First it was our table watching. Then we noticed others were watching too. As Edward's laughter traveled through the room and other sections, people stopped and smiled. Smiles lit the restaurant up as a baby's delight reminded us all of the real reason for Christmas.

Miraculous Interventions™ VIII Extraordinary Miracles

Deborah Aubrey-Peyron

"Look not only for you, but all around the world. My Spirit is moving..."

6 A.M.

(Easter morning 2018)

Dreaming in my telling time.

I saw the earth from high above. It was quiet in the darkness of the outer space. I could feel a presence standing next to me. I was sure it was the angel that usually accompanies me on this walk through the veil of time. I saw the continents. I saw particularly the North American and South American continents. The vast oceans spread out to their shores. In an instant, the scene changed.

The earth broke open like a tremendous earthquake had happened. Out of it, came a brilliant light that shot up to the third heavens. I bent down peering into the darkness to see where it emitted from.

"Wow, uh, that looks like Tennessee. It looks like that light is coming from the south-eastern border of Tennessee."

I thought for only a few seconds.

"I, I believe that is Cleveland, Tennessee! Why that's Cleveland!"

As I spoke those words, great lights split the earth over and over again until it looked like a pin cushion. Lights emanated from all over our planet. It was bathed in a glow that was other-worldly. Simply breathtaking. Revelation hit at once.

"This is the light of Revelation as it goes across the earth one last time."

I could hardly wait to type it up and send it to the good church that we frequent there. I am sure, the best revival yet, will start there.

As if to confirm all of this, I watched a meeting of the church I felt this represented a few days later. The pastor was hot on fire about Cleveland being a hub of the last time revival being there. I knew I had seen their verification in my vision.

The next afternoon I called their office and told the receptionist what I had seen. She asked me to please email everything I could remember about it to them. It sure sounded like verification to her!

Absolutely it was. Get ready church, Jesus is coming back soon!

CHURCH AT THE DOUGLAS INN
IHUB Church
(January 1, 2019)

From 7 a.m. until 8 a.m. I was talking with God. I was reviewing my life in my head. Had all my experiences, all my books I had written in obedience been for naught? Why had I been stopped at every turn? Would things ever pan out? I cried silent tears as Mark slept through it all.

Mark and I woke to daylight. *After* we moaned, we got out of bed, dressed quickly, packed and ran downstairs for a fast breakfast. We were sure we were getting back on the road early, after all we were in a hurry to get home –so much for hurry. We hit the kitchen at 8:40.

While we were eating our meal, a group of young men came into the breakfast area.

Mark immediately said, "I like your shirt!"

I turned around and looked at the young sojourners. Well, he could have been speaking to any one of them!

"Lion Tribe of Judah."

"BBS" with a picture of Jesus on it.

At that I had to ask, "BBS?"

The young man replied with a smile, "Be back soon."

I squealed for effect.

I gave them the five minute version of our story. Two minutes of my birth and three minutes of writing books for Jesus. In a collective, they said, "Wow."

The young man named Corey, who we found out was a seer and a hearer since a child, spoke quietly to Mark. Mark looked at me.

I asked, "What is it? What did he say, Mark?"

Again to Mark, "Your season isn't just yet."

Then he turned to me and said, "God has seen you. He told me to tell you, you are on the right path. It is just not yet. Soon, it is just not yet. Oh, and don't give up."

I dropped my jaw.

He sat there as if listening to an unseen visitor. Cory dropped his head, then nodded, and continued, "Yes, don't stop."

I stammered out, "I didn't get it wrong."

He replied with sincerity, "No! Keep going!"

I simply cried. I knew what his words of encouragement were. I knew why now, it did not matter what time we left that morning.

"Thank you, thank you, thank you!"

Then God spoke to my heart, **"This is why you were here specifically. Why you can't just jump up and leave to go home."**

Cory reached out his hand, "I'm Corey Grippin."

Mark and I smiled. I said, "Nice to meet you young man."

I gave out all the cards I had with me. Just like young people do, they all went looking for me on Facebook. Soon, my phone was pinging away. I responded and friended them. I wrote Corey first.

"Hey Corey! God bless ya, buddy! So very nice to meet you and our other brothers and sisters in Christ Jesus. Have a great year. Mark and I hope God allows our paths to meet again soon! Many blessings, call anytime. Ya'll have friends in Southern Indiana."

Five minutes later, Corey replied.

"It was definitely a divinely orchestrated connection! I get the feeling this was only the start of something bigger. I pray this year is a mind-blowing one for you both!"

Two minutes later I replied.

"Corey Grippin, I agree. And I hope it involves you all too!"

ROBERT & DONNA JACKSON
(Jan. 15, 2019)

Robert Jackson is a good friend and a brother in Christ. I met him on a wonderful group site called "Prophecy Watchers" because we are all prophecy watchers as the days get shorter until the return of our Lord and Savior, Jesus Christ. We have so much in common we kid about being siblings from other mothers. So be it. He always asks about Mark and I always ask about his wife, Donna. Lovely folks, one and all.

Well, I have made no bones about being a seer and clairaudient with our group. Many of them on the site have gifts of the Holy Spirit. But until that day, I was unaware of the gifts Robert possessed until he made confession. One of the most powerful stories in this book, comes from his mouth.

Aren't I glad?

A strong earthquake was reported on the site, "Prophecy Watchers."

Deb: That's getting up there guys! Eeks!

RJ: Deborah Aubrey-Peyron, Sis, I believe the gravity of the moon will have a series effect on our fault lines. I hope my vision does not come true, pray for no major tsunamis.

Deb: Robert Jackson, brother, I know I have visions, I knew Perry Stone has visions. I was not aware you are a visionary. You see visions too?

RJ: Deborah Aubrey-Peyron, about two years ago, I saw a vision of a Tsunami hitting Florida, a huge high wall of water. It really stunned me. On Perry Stone's next broadcast, he talked about it too. I think I may have told you this before, but about 3.5 years ago, Donna and I was visited by an angel in the guise of a loan officer. We sat at the table for hours. She revealed to us Trump would be our next president. Almost a year before he even considered running and revealed a few other things. But she did say there will be a major tsunami hitting the east coast but she did not give a time frame. She did elegantly say Trump is chosen by God and he is the great key to prophecy being fulfilled.

Deb: Wwwwwwwoooowww!!!! Yes you all were visited! I have had two occasions like that myself. Wow! Brother, may I put your story in my next book? These are the kind of stories that the Lord God said He was bringing to fill *Miraculous Interventions VIII*. Call me this evening or at your convenience. Thx so much!

RJ: I just want to add Donna and myself felt the Holy Spirit and without a shadow of a doubt we knew she was an angel. She explained other things that only with supernatural knowledge would know.

Our bodies was tingling when she left.

Deb: Robert Jackson, I bet! Boy have I got two stories for you! This is not a coincidence!

Two nights later, 7 p.m.

Robert Jackson is a 60-year-old artist and sculptor of wood, just as his Scott-Irish great-great-grandfather was. Robert works with a chain saw. He makes animals, faces, bird houses, etc. He does a lot of his woodwork for an Indian Village and museum. Robert's work is sold all over the United States. He worked for Kroger Company for 31 years until he had to go on disability 11 years ago.

He and Donna had married shortly out of high school. Donna has a business with home decorations. It is her passion. She also went to School of Cosmetology. She was a stay-at-home mom for many years to their son and daughter. Two granddaughters are also counted among their fold. All are among the saved in Jesus name.

The first time I called Robert's number it didn't go through. Mark sat beside me at the kitchen table. I had pen and paper in front of me.

Mark said, "Try again."

That time the call went through.

Within seconds, I heard Robert and Donna's voices loud and clear. He had "warned me" that they were just country folks, and I would hear it in their voices. But to me, they sounded a little bit like the South Side of Heaven.

"Deb? Is it you?"

"Robert! Yes it's me! My husband Mark is here with me."

"Hey Mark! How ya doing? This is my wife, Donna."

"Hi Donna!" Mark and I said together.

"Hi ya'll! It's nice to meet you over the phone!" Donna's cheery voice warmed our hearts immediately.

Over the next several minutes, Mark and Robert led conversation. They spoke about West Virginia and the vacations to his grandparents Mark used to take not far from where the Jacksons live. The world seemed smaller and homier the longer the guys talked.

Then the real conversation that I had waited to hear, started.

"Now Robert, I am ready to hear about your angel."

"Well, Deb, this was about three-and-a-half years ago. And there was a tingly presence, an angelic presence around her."

It was the year before Donald Trump had announced he was going to run. No one on earth knew, but the angels in heaven did.

"What was the lady's name?"

"Her name was Mary. She looked to be in her 40's. She had a spray of silver in her long, black hair. She had dark eyes, petite and very soft spoken. And she was a loan officer."

"What time of the year was it?" I asked.

"It was May, early spring of 2015. She came to our house early in the morning. She just started talking about what was happening in the world and the biblical implications of it all. She said in this world people needed an intervention. Someone who would stand up for good people. That was when she said that Donald Trump would run for president and win. At the time we didn't know he was a professed Christian. But now we know. Trump is armored and clothed. They can't get to him. God prepared him for this the last 10 to 20 years."

"Wow," I breathed. "Is that the way your meeting started?"

Robert went on.

"No. Mary showed up with the papers for our loan application. But Donna and I both knew as she stepped into our home, she had a presence about her. She had a calming, knowledgeable presence about her. She wrapped up the material part of our conversation for the bank very quickly. Then she very quickly changed the conversation to the Bible. She talked about the same things we believed that would come to pass. She informed us on Biblical events."

Mark and I were taken aback by all that the two of them had to say. We couldn't believe our ears.

"Deb, we knew we were sitting with an angel! The meeting was between an hour-and-a-half to two-and-a-half hours long. The loan was just a small part of it. Mary went through the events that were happening now in scripture. She came in, introduced herself, helped with the papers for the loan, and closed her book. Then started talking about prophecy and Donald Trump. She said the Bible says the Last Trump will sound. Mary kept saying it isn't a coincidence that Donald Trump will be the next president. She said it several times. Then she said things in the future."

"Oh my!"

"There is going to be a great calamity. A wall of water, a tsunami will devastate, flood all the way to Roanoke, Virginia. The only thing that will stop them is the Great Smokies."

My heart felt sick with anticipation of the events spoken of. We have children and grandchildren in harm's way. A long with about 80 million other people.

Robert began again, "Even scientists are talking about Super Blood Moons, the pull of gravity on the earth's plates--how they will move. When she spoke about the great earthquake and tsunami she did not put a time frame on it."

"She also mentioned the verse with the trumpet, the '67 war in Israel. God sent to the Rabbis a device to make and they made it by instructions by Yeshua. When they were overwhelmed, the priests called for the device to activate, and a special sound went out. As it went forth, their enemy dropped their rifles and ran screaming. When they were captured, they asked them to make it stop. They told the soldiers when they heard the sound, they saw flaming angels next to the Israeli army and took off running."

"Holy cow." I whistled. "Donald Trump was chosen by Yeshua Himself for this time." I whispered, "I believe you."

Robert went on, "Then Mary asked me a question."

"Wow, what?"

"She asked me why I feel like, after 1,000 year reign, why the Lord lets the devil come back. Robert paused as we considered the question.

He replied, "God gives everyone a chance to choose either way. The people that are born during the 1,000 years will have to choose God or satan. These choices are for the people that do not have their glorified bodies and choose to be born again or die with satan. It must be their final choice. Mary told me that was a very good answer."

Robert got quiet for a few minutes as if thinking something over to tell me.

"Two years ago, in 2016, I saw the East Coast in a vision. I pictured Florida as plain as day. I saw a tsunami totally take Florida out. It is coming. Then I heard the sound of shofars and horns. I heard trumpets in the Eastern sky. I was in my workshop at my desk. I put my foot on the step and felt instantly close to the Lord. When I walked in my house, I felt the presence of the Holy Spirit. I bowed and knelt. I was not scared. It was peaceful, unexplainable."

"Glorious."

"Mary also said Trump would surround himself with good Christians and knowledge. And she said Trump may be the last president. During his presidency the Last Trumpet will sound. It will be the end. Donna and I are praying for another four year term. I think he will win and toward his last four years, all will come to a head. In our last lingering years revival will come."

"The last thing Mary said was time is short."

As Robert spoke those words, my mind wandered to the time the angel had told me time was short. And the time that Andy was told by his friend that had gone to heaven, that time was short. It was my third verification.

As I pondered these thoughts, Robert spoke about his father, a Pentecostal. Robert spoke about his gifts to be able to see and hear and listen. Once he asked his mom why him.

She replied, "It was meant to be. Dreams and visions."

Robert and Donna are humble people. I am proud to know them and call them family. Robert is gifted with understanding when he hears.

Finally Donna spoke up.

"Deb?"

"Yes, ma'am?"

"We are so glad to have met you. We can relate to you. You won't think we're crazy. It is so good to know and hear knowledge. To know the truth is out there."

"You are most welcome."

Robert piped in. "Can I ask you somethin'?"

"Sure!"

"Do you think that America is Mystery Babylon?"

Before I could answer, Mark spoke up as if on cue. Mark said, "No. That's Mecca."

Robert replied, "There are great arguments on both sides. But I'm leaning in Mark's favor."

Donna said, "I think America is close to it."

Robert went on, "The antichrist will be from Rome, the city of the seven hills."

I spoke of the dream I had on Easter of 2018 at 5:30 a.m. About the earthquake and the great light that reached to the third heaven. Robert said he was told in the spirit I am a warrior.

Robert spoke of his father who was a Pentecostal Evangelist for 30 years. He asked Robert many questions. When he is asked, answers come to him. Robert felt like he and I are gifted.

Mark told about the spirit of corruption that was on America. We need to repent and pray against it. And to pray for discernment. Robert said he already prays hard for it.

By the end of the meeting with Mary, Robert and Donna had to pick their chins up off the floor. They had been overwhelmed by the presence of an angel. They had been visited. As Mary left for the door, she turned around and gave them one final word. She told Donna to remember these things. "Everything will be alright. Don't worry." Then she hugged her and Robert, then she was gone. Peace fell over their household and they shouted and praised Jesus!

Now, the warning had sounded. After telling me their story, Robert's burden had been lifted.

Mine had begun.

READIED FOR HEAVEN
(Third week of December, 2019)

DREAM

I was out with my friend Katie, shopping. All of a sudden we heard a noise coming from above us. We looked up. As we looked up, we were being lifted off the ground. I reached for Katie to hold hands and could not quite get to her.

The higher we went the faster we flew. As darkness surrounded me, I saw all of my sinful times in my life. I had great sorrow and cried as they flashed before me.*

By the time we arrived at our destination, a place brilliant white, I was standing in a gown with no spot or blemish.

A little later that morning, I called Katie to let her know I dreamed about her. When I got to the point where I was seeing my sins before me and crying, Katie began to shout.

"Oh, Deb!" Katie cried. "Do you understand what that means? As you were heading towards Heaven, your sins fell off of you. You were being readied for Heaven.*"

Oh thank God.

* *This would be Purgatory -- editor*

Full versions of each book sampled in this edition is available at Amazon.com or at HomeCraftedArtisty.com via links to Amazon.

Miraculous Interventions Books ISBN Numbers:
"Best of the Miraculous Interventions™ Series"
ISBN-13: 978 0 9893714 0 7

"Miraculous Interventions™
ISBN-13: 978 0 9893714 9 0

"Miraculous Interventions™ II: Modern Day Priests, Prophets, Pastors and Everyday Visionaries"
ISBN 13: 978 0 9893714 9 0

"Miraculous Interventions™ III: 2012 The Miraculous Year" ISBN 13: 978 0 9964089 3 6

"Miraculous Interventions™ IV The Gathering"
ISBN 13: 978 0 9964089 9 8

Miraculous Interventions™ V: The Small, Still Voice
ISBN 13: 978 0 9974347 4 3

Miraculous Interventions™ VI, Warn Those Who Will Listen
ISBN 13: 978 0 9974347 6 7

Miraculous Interventions™ VII, The Saving of America
ISBN 13: 978 0 9974347 7 4

Miraculous Interventions™ VIII, Extraordinary Miracles
ISBN 13: 978 1 7323437 7 1
Best of Miraculous Interventions™ Series *[Books I – IV]*
ISBN 13: 978-0-9893714-5-2
Best of Miraculous Interventions™ Books V - VIII
ISBN 13: 978-1-7323437-9-5